Parenting Teen Girls in
Today's Challenging World

Proven Methods for Improving
Teenagers Behaviour with Whole
Brain Training

Bukky Ekine-Ogunlana

Published by
TCEC Publishing
TCEC House
14-18 Ada Street, London Fields,
E8 4QU, England, Great Britain.

Table of Contents

DEDICATION

This book is dedicated to our three amazing children and all the beautiful children all over the world who over the years have passed through the T.C.E.C 6-16 years programme. Thank you for the opportunity to serve you and invest in your colourful and bright future.

Editor's Preface

Whether you are a first-time parent to a daughter, or you've been here before, parenting girls takes patience, compassion, and love, just as it would for your son. However, girls have a different experience than boys and have to face a slew of barriers and hurdles that will come as they age. Devising a parenting technique to raise confident and strong-willed daughters can be difficult because parents, especially new parents, do not know where to begin. But do not fret! This Is precisely the reason that has driven the motivations to write this book. It is dedicated to parents everywhere who mean well and want the best for their children but feel like they are completely in, over their heads. A good thing to remember is that many parents share this feeling, but they can overcome this through perseverance and patience.

One thing to remember and always keep at the back of your mind is that parenting eventually becomes mostly instinctual. As much as you want to adhere to the tips outlined in this book, the best course of action is to absorb the knowledge presented in this book and bring it into your real life as you parent your children, regardless of what age they are. And as they continue to age and mature, it is essential to learn how to adapt and change with them.

The ideas presented in this book are general rules you can choose to apply to your life when parenting your children. From toddlers to teens, the tips presented in this book serve as assurances for parents unsure of what method to employ in their own lives. Ultimately, these methods are rooted in compassion and empathy. But the crucial thing to know is that every child is uniquely different. As I'm sure you have noticed within your child, every girl and every boy has varying perceptions of life and meets life's challenges differently. Discipline comes in many forms, and educating your children is not as universal as it might seem. Every child will experience their trials and tribulations that will shape them into a unique person. As a result, parents have to understand this, and parenting has to reflect this accordingly.

You may find that some of the tips in this book do not apply to your child. More often than not, parenting takes trial and error. Parents sometimes forget this important detail and feel frustrated and demotivated when pushing their children down the right path. Instilling discipline, compassion, empathy, and kindness within children does not simply happen overnight. Parenting is a lifelong journey that never truly ends. So, the biggest tip that I can impart to any reader is to treat your children with respect and love that is never compromised. This is the foundational basis for good parenting.

This book is a must-read for prospective parents who are afraid of the unknown. It will set you up for a bright future ahead that prioritizes your children and their well-being. Parenting is a bumpy road, and you will experience extreme highs and the lowest of lows.

This is all part of the journey that every parent encounters. This book will help you reflect on your choices in an intentional and meaningful way.

For parents who are deep in parenting trials, the ideas presented here will help you regain confidence in your abilities. It will help you turn around your situation for the better, especially if you are dealing with children who are acting out or going through a difficult time themselves.

Ultimately, this book serves to help parents provide the best possible environment for their children.

Introduction

While it is difficult to say if one gender is inherently more problematic to raise than the other, being a girl and more specifically, a teenage girl can be a tough and challenging time as the female body experiences extreme changes that can undoubtedly scare and even traumatize young girls. Many biological differences can affect both boys and girls, and for girls, hormonal changes can significantly impact a female's mental health and wellbeing. Additionally, societal expectations on the role of females limit them as they age. Females are subjected to glass ceilings and several biases that males will never understand.

For parents raising teenage girls, this can be a breeze for many as girls tend to be more resourceful and independent at this age than their male counterparts. However, that isn't to say that all girls are this way, and it certainly depends on the environment they are raised in and the childhood influences that play a massive part in shaping teens and their later years. Parents are faced with the typical teenage woes and have to deal with the set of problems that come with being a teenage boy or a teenage girl. In general, for adolescent girls, the social norm that has been established allows them to ask for help or receive help and affection. Facing emotional issues tends to be a more common problem seen in teenage boys.

So, when it comes to raising boys and girls, techniques catered to specific genders simply do not exist because the issues that each gender deals with can be so diverse and unique to each individual. Rather than seeing teen girls and boys in groups and adhering to stereotypes that make sweeping generalizations about how they may act, the more effective way is to see your child as an individual and treat them as such. This way, you can better understand the issues they may be facing and cater to their needs.

Seasoned parents would argue that teenagerhood is the most challenging time for parenting. Many parents might say that this period for your teenagers is a time of high emotions and added pressure as your teenager experience leaving their childhood and are on the cusp of adulthood. Your teens are in the process of making big decisions that will affect their futures, particularly with their educations and careers, which is an incredibly stressful time for most. Teens could be experiencing more complex relationships and the emotions associated with that. Additionally, as your children age, they become more accustomed to the fact that the world is more flawed than what they might have been used to during their protected childhood years that featured a far more idealistic and optimistic view. As your children age, they are met with the responsibilities they will have to take on as adults. With all of these in mind, the immense stress that can weigh on a teen's mental health during this time can be enormous. With this age transition being so formative and crucial for your teens, the same stress and pressure reflect on parents, which is why teenagehood is challenging for both parents and children alike.

However, that is not to say that techniques don't exist for raising respectable and good-hearted teens. It comes down to parents instilling these good values into their teens to carry these life lessons well into adulthood and practice them. As much as gender stereotyping should be discouraged, there are a few inherent differences between boys and girls that should be differentiated and discussed when raising girls and boys. However, keep in mind that all of the tips introduced in these books are interchangeable between genders and can be applied to any teen. They have no prerequisites or preconditions that need to be followed before being applied. These tips are universally applicable and really serve to nurture your teen's interests and needs, regardless of their gender.

These books are here to provide a framework for raising your teens. They are great resources to understand what your child may be going through during this especially volatile time. Refer to this books companion piece if you are raising a son and seek to understand the challenges they may face.

After reading this guide, please feel free to leave a review based on your findings and how useful the guide was to you. I would be incredibly thankful if you could take 60 seconds to write a brief review on the platform of purchase, even if it's just a few sentences!

Chapter 1:
Raising Teenage Daughters

Raising teenage daughters does not necessarily have to be a tricky thing. What becomes problematic is establishing the balance between the parent and child dynamic because of the inherent need to be an authoritative figure while maintaining a close connection with your daughter. Striking this balance is essential and one of the biggest challenges that parents face when raising their teenage daughters because of the extreme changes they are going through. While parents have to discover the best way to parent their kids, they also have to evolve alongside them and accept that times are changing where their children seek to be more independent by their terms during this stage of their lives. While their bodies are changing, so are their minds. Parents have to deal with the fact that their children simply do not require them as much as they did when they were younger and more reliant on them for their survival. This is the time for them to start dipping their toes in the water and finding their way through the challenges of life.

Your kids must learn things by themselves and avoid feeding them the answers to everything.

While your teenage daughter is growing, the emotional impact that puberty has on a girl should not be underestimated. You will see changes manifest in many different ways, or perhaps even a combination of all of the following. Girls tend to be significantly underestimated, and their emotions tend to be brushed off because of the stereotypes that encourage a mindset that females are too emotional. Not only is this a dangerous mindset, but it also wholly sweeps all of the issues your daughter may be going through under the rug. It is essential to be perceptive of the changes they may be going through because they may not be immediately comfortable sharing these private details with you. It is equally important to listen to them and validate their feelings and act on them if they need help. Some parents may struggle with trying to identify if their daughter may be going through a hard time. Here are some signs to look out for if you suspect your teenage daughter is experiencing difficulty.

1. Changing tides

Physical developments and changes that puberty brings can trigger body and self-esteem issues for your teenage daughter. It is not uncommon for self-consciousness to manifest during this period as teens experience acne discomfort and other changes to their appearance. This can trigger a lifetime of harmful or self-destructive behaviour if not taken seriously from the get-go.

2. Mood swings

While TV shows and movies depict an often exaggerated and cliched version of how teenage daughters face mood swings, there is some truth to the stereotype as teen girls tend to show more varying degrees of sadness and happiness levels throughout their daily lives as societal expectations allow girls to be more expressive of their emotions and feelings. At the same time, males do not experience this in the same way.

3. Independence

Puberty does not just entail biological changes. As teenagerhood is a time to express independence, this can manifest in many different ways. Some girls may choose to dress differently and express themselves through their fashion. Some may decide to try out other hobbies or activities. The possibilities here are endless.

4. Body image

Body image impacts teen girls especially more profoundly and girls tend to focus on their outward appearances because of how drastic the changes can be. Additionally, the constant presence and availability of social media and edited pictures circulating the internet and have become commonplace create unrealistic expectations of beauty for young girls to aspire towards.

5. Friendships

Friend groups, particularly among girls, can sometimes be especially volatile. There is some truth in the stereotype of girls flocking in cliques. Your daughter may be on the receiving end of the negative aspect and might be experiencing loneliness or even alienation from their social circles. Knowing how your child is doing socially is especially crucial during these formative years because it can significantly leave a lasting negative impact if left unattended.

6. Relationships

At this age, teenagers may be acting on romantic impulses and experiencing their first loves and consequently, their first heartbreaks. I have seen these many times in the schools. This can be an extremely vulnerable time that may result in them going through difficult emotions as they grapple with new relationships and the pressures associated with a relationship. Good counselling and guide have helped in school and could benefit at home as well.

7. Bullying

Bullying can manifest in many forms during a teen's life. It can profoundly impact your teen's personality and behaviour that can follow them well into adulthood if not dealt with appropriately early on.

8. Peer Pressure

During this time, teens want to feel like they belong and are part of a group and identify with the people around them. But peer pressure can introduce its stresses and put your teens into uncomfortable situations that they might not be sure how to get out of.

9. Substance Use

Drugs and alcohol make themselves more known during this period of your teen's life. Peer pressure can play a massive impact in this as your teen might find themselves back into a corner where they feel like they have to try these dangerous substances. Or they may rely on alcohol or drugs to relieve the stress they may be experiencing.

10. Mental health

Whatever the cause may be, your teen's mental health will be impacted in some way during their most formative years. It can manifest in several negative ways, from social anxiety to depression. There are plenty of things that can affect a teen's mental health; from friends and social interactions, break up, parental pressures, academic pressures...the list goes on.

Chapter 2:
Effective Ways to Help Your Teens Cope

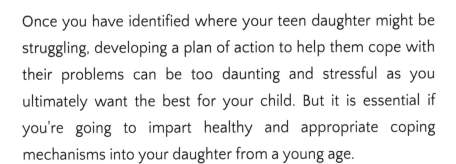

Once you have identified where your teen daughter might be struggling, developing a plan of action to help them cope with their problems can be too daunting and stressful as you ultimately want the best for your child. But it is essential if you're going to impart healthy and appropriate coping mechanisms into your daughter from a young age.

1. Self-image

The issues that arise out of self-image issues can be diverse and extreme. It can manifest in the form of eating disorders and body dysmorphia. While boys can also go through the same thing, girls experience an added pressure on their outward appearance during their teenage years. To cope with this, monitor your teen closely, especially at the dinner table. Notice their eating habits and make sure that they are getting plenty of fruits and vegetables. Have an open communication line to discuss how Photoshop can significantly alter how females look and that a person's worth is not based on how they look. Instil in them that being healthy is ultimately the most important thing.

Teach your daughter the importance of self-worth by encouraging her to have positive role models in her life. Positive role models could be anyone, from parents to teachers to friends. These models exist in their lives and show them how to cope with situations like growing up and facing the changes they are experiencing. Growing up, you get to figure out who you are by what other people tell you that you are until you begin to discover for yourself who you are.

One effective method to help your daughter with the way she views herself is to be cautious with the words you use around her.

It is more difficult for us as humans to place a lens on ourselves. Instead, what often happens is that our attitudes project onto another person. In this case, as parents continue to project a negative outlook, our children reflect this same negative attitude. And even when we look at the mirror, we tend to confirm what we have heard other people say about us. An excellent way to understand this is in the scenario of when someone tells you, "You have particles of food on your mouth". The immediate response here is to go to a mirror and check your reflection. When you notice that the food particles are there, your response is usually to remove it because the mirror has identified the problem you did not see by yourself.

Teens tend to approach mirrors with the opinion of others already ingrained in their minds. As adults, we have grown and matured to develop our views of ourselves. Still, young girls take everything said about them to that mirror and scrutinize themselves down to the smallest details to see if it is true, especially when it comes to negative comments. Even if it is not valid, they will look and look until they start to see what may not even be there. So, what can you do to help?

Speak scriptures, encouraging and uplifting words to your daughter. I am not just talking about the usual "you look beautiful today" because focusing solely on their looks teaches them to value themselves based on their appearances. Instead, please focus on the good habits and values they exhibit, such as hard work, persistence, and diligence. Notice how caring and creative they are and be sure to point out these strengths.

The critical thing to remember is that your words are the seeds that they take to the mirror. As they take it to the mirror, they will reconsider your comments, and their understanding of who they are continues to develop positively. When they go outside of the home environment, they may not receive good seeds (words) from others, where the real test lies. However, having the foundation of hearing positive and uplifting words from home will help them differentiate between what they can accept as true and false. Teens will begin to see that not everything everyone says about them is correct. Most teen girls do not know this, and it will be helpful to let them know the truth.

2. Relationship

This can be an exceptionally complicated thing to relate to your children because young love we see in schools can be innocent yet also problematic in its way. Especially from an adult's perspective, trying to relate to your teenage daughter's experiences can be doubly challenging, but this is the time to educate your teenage daughter on sex. Sex Education should by no means be a taboo subject because you want to be able to impart on her the importance of keeping herself. While schools have health subjects, it is important to teach her biological processes and give her a basic understanding of how pregnancy can happen. Be open and honest and share with her without sugar-coating things and do not treat this subject as taboo because it will be a sign to her to bottle up her feelings and feel ashamed. The absolute last thing you want for your daughter is to be ashamed and have a lifelong regret for making her own independent decisions.

When it comes to the area of relationships at a teenager's level, where do we even begin? Many parents think that talking with girls at a young age is enough to ensure that they will grow and continue developing as they deem it correct. However, parents must be more sensitive and in-tune with their teens' feelings and emotions in this modern age. There are two ways to which this conversation might go: it could be either too awkward for all the parties involved or just another simple conversation between a family.

One of the best ways to approach a subject of this magnitude is by highlighting it in its natural setting. For example, this can include bringing up the topic of friendships with boys after seeing your teen in a social environment and with that as the jumping-off point. You can branch out into a more in-depth conversation. The aim here is to inform your child of certain boundaries while also understanding their relationships at a romantic capacity.

For many mothers and their daughters, this conversation ends up being difficult because it can lead to a lot of embarrassment from both parties. But the reality is that the conversation needs to be had. Making this a taboo subject only closes doors for open discussion and talks.

3. Bullying

This can be a challenging subject for your daughter to broach because of a myriad of reasons. They may feel ashamed or scared of the consequences. They may think that bullying is their fault and may not understand that they do not deserve to be bullied. Ensure that you have a strong foundation with your daughter to recognize if she is shutting down or being more closed-off. This can be an indication that she is being bullied. Broaching the subject with her can be difficult. She may not feel comfortable sharing the details but reassuring her that you will support her and try your best to help her out of this challenging situation can significantly ease the stress. Give her advice on how to face bullying and stand up for herself. If the issue is more severe, it may be time to step in and have a serious talk with her school. This is where parents come in and directly intervene with your child's time at school and have a serious discussion with the teacher. Sometimes having proof might even help the case. If this is an instance of cyberbullying, saving screenshots to show to the administration and authorities (if need be) can help further the issue from just a reprimand to more severe punishment to the perpetrator.

4. Education

Teenagerhood can be a doubly stressful time for your kids' education because they are inching closer and closer to college and university. This added pressure can significantly affect your child's performance, and more often than not, children can feel like their self-worth is tied to the grades they get. To tackle this, reassuring your child that you value hard work and effort more so than grades. Low grades are not an indicator of any person's self-worth and consider finding an outlet for your child to engage in to destress and relax after school.

While watching your child struggling is difficult, simply handing them the answers is even worse. Don't be overprotective over your daughters and let them make mistakes. A big part of developing a resilient sense of self-worth is the ability to bounce back from the obstacles that life presents. So, the next time your daughter is struggling to cram for an exam she had weeks to study for, don't merely bail her out and give her the easy way out. Allow her to learn from her mistakes and face the ramifications of her errors, which, as she will learn, does not mean that everything comes crashing down. Facing the consequences and overcoming challenges is part of becoming a resilient adult. Differentiate between being her support system and someone who simply cleans up her messes.

5. The power of "no."

It is also crucial to educate your daughter, above all else, the power of the word "no". Saying "no" can help your daughter out of situations and can even save her life. Your daughter has every right to say "no", especially when she is uncomfortable, and while all parents would agree with this, many do not enforce this enough with their daughters. Prioritize teaching them this in their development. Your teens may need to practice this a few times with their family members to get comfortable with the idea of asserting their feelings but doing so is an excellent way to get accustomed to politely but firmly refusing someone.

6. Substance Use

Educate your kids about the detrimental side effects of drugs and alcohol, in addition to the consequences they face from illegal consumption as they are underage. Some teens in a discussion in the class argued that the best way to combat this is to allow them to experience it in a controlled environment, like under their parent's supervision. (The first trial is the only trial needed to be addicted)

Teen girls are more vulnerable to developing alcohol and drug problems due to their greater susceptibility to peer pressure. Their surroundings and environmental stress is often the cause that leads teen girls to succumb to substance usage. Teen girls tend to turn to substances to cope with existing issues. Pay close attention to their moods to see if anything has changed or if they appear any different. Drastic mood changes can indicate that your teen is experimenting with drugs or alcohol. If you suspect so, take action immediately from a professional as their health and safety could be at risk.

Chapter 3:
Parenting Teenage Girls

These techniques can be interchangeable with parenting teen boys as parenting, in general, requires being compassionate and empathetic to your child's struggles. These tips are a great place to start if you are unsure how to transition from raising a young girl to an adolescent. Ultimately, there is no "one size fits all" approach for raising a son or daughter, and it may take some trial and error to find the perfect fit of balancing discipline and being their friend. Here are some tips for dealing with the challenges that raising a teenager can bring:

1. Communication is key

A lot of grief can be saved if your children simply communicate what they may be going through. But this just is not the case because of the complexities of emotions your teens are faced with. They might feel scared or intimidated and fear punishment or shame if they were to share their true feelings, which means that it falls onto the parent to connect with their teens as much as possible and be an avid listener. Establish yourself as a trusted confidant and a safe space to share their deepest and darkest concerns.

Cindy and her daughter Lilly shared a close bond ever since Lilly was young. During Lilly's teen years, her mother's relationship suffered because she found herself developing new interests that differed from her mother's. This was difficult for Cindy because she had grown so used to Lilly's companionship as her daughter and friend. Communication lines that were once wide open diminished every day as Lilly grew increasingly secretive with her new friends in high school and the new things that interested her in life. She simply did not want to share with her mother what she and her friends were up to.

For Cindy, re-establishing communication was the challenge she had to face. Through trial and error, she did so by finding a new hobby for her and her daughter to pursue. Gardening became a hobby of choice. What first felt like manual labour to Lilly turned into a period she looked forward to every weekend to spend time with just her and her mother. Cindy was initially met with a lot of resistance as Lilly said she would rather spend time with her friends than with her mother. While the words were extremely hurtful, Cindy knew not to take it to heart. She knew that teens said things that they regretted and making mistakes was part of life. And she was validated when the next day Lilly came to apologize for her harsh words. Cindy had established trust and respect from Lilly's early days as a child, and here it was blossoming right before her eyes.

The fact is that Lilly had simply grown out of the hobbies she had loved to do with her mother. This was where Cindy realized that as a parent to a growing child, a teen no less, you might have to adapt and change as your child does to keep up with them. While Lilly loved doing the hobbies like cooking and baking as a child, she no longer liked them and found that this was the basis of her relationship with her mother, which is why she continuously pushed away from her as she aged and entered high school.

Once Cindy established a new neutral zone, it took some time for Lilly to recognize that her mother ultimately cared about her and was not someone who was going to judge her. By Cindy maintaining the boundaries between herself and Lilly and not being too pushy, she was able to get Lilly to open up after a few weeks of gardening together. She found out that Lilly struggled with insecurities and found difficulty coping with school and the new friends she was making. Being able to open up to her mother was crucial, and she realized how big of a hole it had left when she didn't have her mother to rely on and always pushed her away.

While parents may have strong and solid foundations established with their children that they anticipate will always be in place, this certainly isn't the case. The truth is that these foundations can be knocked down if you aren't paying attention. Details in behaviour and attitude can be a massive giveaway to how your child is doing if you pay attention and know what to look for. This means that you have to be wise to your child all the time. Sometimes communication lines can go out, so it is up to parents to figure out how to rewire the connection lines to get their kids to open up to them again. This takes a lot of patience and trust, but with a solid foundation, your kids will eventually come around.

2. Establish rules

Having realistic and logical boundaries that are concise and age-appropriate is crucial during this stage because teens want to challenge everything around them as they experience independence for the first time in their lives. Always expect that your rules will be broken, so be prepared with age-appropriate consequences that will teach your teens a lesson in a sustainable and effective way.

The punishments you dole out to your children will differ as they age. For example, if your child demonstrated lousy behaviour as a toddler, a common punishment that suited this was a time-out in the corner or perhaps taking away a privilege like watching TV. As a teen, time-outs definitely won't have the same effect. You might succeed in humiliating your teenager, but this will only develop even more resentment and foster frustration towards you. Instead, a parent to a teen might take a more "adult" approach to the time-out by perhaps cutting your teens curfew and making it earlier or banning them from using electronic devices. Taking away privileges as a punishment is an effective way to get through to your kids because it effectively forces them to listen to you when the things they enjoy are in jeopardy.

The tricky part is setting boundaries itself. Setting overcomplicated boundaries will only succeed in forcing your kid to ignore them and go about their way. For example, contradicting yourself and continuously changing the rules will eventually wear your child down so much that they choose to ignore the rules you have set. Avoid doing so by discussing boundaries with your children before setting them. Getting them involved in the process is an excellent way to gauge their expectations and how you can still respect their wishes and form a fair compromise for everyone involved. For example, curfews are a contentious subject for teens because while they want to stay out as late as possible, parents are expected to stay up waiting for their kids to return home. The expectation there is unfair towards parents and everyone else in the household. So in this case, coming to a compromise about a reasonable curfew is an excellent way to make sure that your teens both respect it and adhere to it.

3. Don't take bad attitudes and behaviour personally

As much as your teen's words can hurt and cut deep, try your best not to take it personally. This does not mean that they will not receive consequences for being disrespectful but be prepared to be argued with and have your buttons pushed continuously as your teens test the boundaries and fight against any form of authority or control.

4. Healthy risks

While children are attracted to pushing the boundaries and taking risks, this can be performed healthily. Through travelling, physical challenges and new social situations, there are plenty of ways to take healthy risks without endangering themselves or their health. Furthermore, parents have a better understanding of what their children might be up to when they engage in these activities, which significantly eases the mind. Encouraging these activities also broadens your child's horizons and diversifies their experiences and exposes them to many new and healthy coping ways.

5. Compromise

As much as you have a developed relationship with your teens and try your best to create a parenting style that fits them best, sometimes you might have to compromise with your teen's whims that may seem outlandish. Sometimes you may have to accept that this is another way for them to express themselves during this time. While you cannot control every single outcome, finding a happy medium and compromising with your teen is a way to try and maintain some semblance of calm and happiness.

6. Express love and affection

Unconditional love is precisely that. Your children will continuously make mistakes and push the boundaries, and you will as well as you try to help them navigate through their lives and face the challenges that will be presented. No one has the perfect answer or response to everything. What is crucial is that you take these mistakes and turn them into learning lessons for your kids to set an example of how to respond to situations of extreme emotions appropriately. Likewise, the backbone of everything you do when raising children is to practice unconditional love. This should not be leveraged or withheld because your child is exhibiting frustration or challenging behaviours.

7. Express how you feel

As your teens are older and more mature, they can relate to the emotions you may be feeling more so than they would have as a child. Being open and vulnerable to your children can significantly encourage them to do the same when trying to understand what they are going through. By sharing your struggles, your children can see that adults make mistakes and are susceptible to challenges. Being open with your kids encourages them to want to share more because you are setting a clear example of sharing their feelings and avoiding bottling them up. This can eventually implode and lead to unhealthy ways of coping and mental health issues like depression and anxiety.

8. Be compassionate

Your teen is experiencing struggles that to you may seem minute, but for them can be astronomical. Be compassionate to their struggles and try not to judge them too harshly as a young age tends to be a slew of bad decision making and reckless behaviour. Try and think of how you thought when you were that age look how far you have come in your thinking and understanding they too are yet to make that same journey. Instead, provide them with the support they need; whether it's a shoulder to cry on or someone to keep them company while they go through the consequences they face.

9. You won't always be right

Accept when you are wrong. Parents often struggle with this because they are so accustomed to telling their kids specifically what to do, and they may be met with resistance as they age and enter adolescence. Take time to evaluate the situation, and sometimes, you may be wrong too. It is far more effective and commendable to admit when you are wrong, as painful as it may be when you are in the face of an argument with your child, but it is the right thing to do.

10. Trust their judgement

As difficult as it may be relinquishing your hold on your kids, it is a natural consequence of your children growing up. When this happens, give them the freedom to act on their own choices and trust that they are making the most informed choice. Parents often want to step in and tell their kids exactly what to do, but should they make a mistake, it turns into a learning lesson for them to take with them for the next time and the rest of your life.

11. Choose your battles

It is true that raising teens bring a lot of butting heads and arguments. Sometimes you have to let it be. Picking a fight every single time is not only frustrating for both parent and child, but it can also encourage teens to want to rebel even more as your rules get stricter and increasingly tight. Pick your battles wisely and save yourself another day of arguments and fighting. Sometimes allowing your teens to decide things for themselves as long as they are not harming themselves or those around them is a way of compromising with the fact that they are growing up and making their own choices.

12. Focus on positivity

Positive encouragement is a tried-and-true method to get your kids to feel more confident in themselves. Especially when your child is going through a hard time, this can be a reminder that not all moments will be challenging and emotionally draining.

Spending time with family and friends or pursuing their hobbies can give them a break from stressors and temporarily give teens a chance to focus on something else, rather than constantly obsessing over the issue at hand. If it's an appropriate time, try to encourage your teen to get away from the chaos and focus on something that they love to do to briefly take their minds off of things and help them clear their heads. While this is not a way to completely solve problems, it relieves stress, impacting overall mental health.

13. Recognize their rights

Parents often view their children as young and impressionable, which causes them to indulge their kids, even as they are in their teenage years. This stunts their development and fosters resentment as children do not feel seen or heard as individuals because they are continually being treated as children and not being given the freedoms they feel like they deserve. Recognize that your children are growing up and that they deserve freedoms in this process. They are no longer babies whose every move has to be tended to and watched. Allowing your kids to explore the world on their own enables them to grow and flourish in their way.

14. Respect goes both ways

While you expect your teens to respect you as an authority figure, respect their choices as well. Particularly during their teen years, your child may experiment and dabble in a new identity, whether that is through fashion or their interests. It can manifest in many ways. Frustration can build when parents choose not to validate this new identity. While it may be a phase, it can also potentially not be. Treat your kids with the same respect that you expect for yourself. Respect their choices and understand that you may not like everything they do, and they will not always turn to you for advice. Despite this, you should not hold a grudge or treat them any lesser than they are.

15. Professional help

Consider speaking to a professional if you find that you cannot grasp what your teen might be going through, whether it is because of reluctance on your teen's part to share or if the issue is more severe than you can help her manage. There is no shame in seeking professional help because it gives your teen a neutral party to speak to who provides a safe, judgement-free space for them to express themselves. This does not mean you are any less of a parent; it makes you a commendable one for recognizing your strengths and weaknesses and ultimately placing your child's health over your ego. Many parents struggle with the blow that their ego faces for they believe that speaking to a professional means that they are not a good parent. This is definitely not the case. Many teens recognize their parents' limitations and appreciate the degree of seriousness they treat their mental health.

Siblings are an essential subject that should be discussed when it comes to raising teenagers. Your child's siblings play a huge role in shaping and moulding them into the person they are, alongside your influence as a parent. For parents with multiple children, the dynamic in your household is one of the most important things. A dynamic that is not balanced will be met with a lot of chaos. This might look like one child getting more attention than the other or one child getting more leniency than their sibling. The list goes on and on. Without striking a balance between all the siblings, you risk breaking down the foundations that you worked so tirelessly to build among all your children.

Mina was a mother of two before becoming a mother to three children very unexpectedly. Her goddaughter Rosie entered into the family's lives without much warning, throwing the entire family dynamic out of balance because Mina's children Anna and Leah now had a new sibling. With more children meant less time divided between each of them. The beginning stages of the family was rough as they tried to make Rosie's unexpected appearance work. As happy and thrilled as they were about gaining a new daughter, Mina and her husband Jeremy were concerned about money becoming tighter now that they had another mouth to feed. While they never let it show and provided for all their children with as much joy and love as they could, their financial troubles were weighing them down. But Jeremy and Mina agreed never to tell their children and burden them with adult problems.

However, Anna, Leah, and Rosie were perceptive of their parents and could see that they were under a great deal of stress. But despite acknowledging this, Anna and Leah found it increasingly difficult to spend time with their parents as they once had. They were always working, and if they weren't, they were helping Rosie with something or another. On the other hand, Rosie was going through a rough patch as she had to very abruptly leave her old life behind and permanently join her godparents' family.

Families tend to go through a struggle in the beginning as they attempt to figure things out. In Mina's family's case, the battle was doubly difficult as they were dealing with a new addition to their family, financial troubles and trying to have all of the siblings bond together at the same time. Jealousy was bound to brew, and that is precisely what happened.

Rosie was experiencing difficulty herself as she attempted to join the family while dealing with her past trauma of leaving her home abruptly to join a new one that felt hostile from her new siblings. She made constant comments about being maltreated compared to the family's birth children and Shut down emotionally and refused to share her feelings.

The issues seemed to be compounding until everything finally came to a head one day that forced an entire family intervention. Mina and Jeremy were able to identify that the family dynamics had been compromised and were not getting any better. No one was benefiting from this family dynamic because no one felt supported or cared for. Everyone was more concerned with their issues and continued to retreat into their corners instead of bringing people closer. The problems were immense and unsolvable in one day.

The good news is that the issues were solved over the next few months. The family dynamic was altered to which everyone was now supportive of one another. No one felt neglected because everyone was able to voice their concerns honestly and without any filters. By doing so, Mina and Jeremy's household was a lot calmer for everyone involved. Eventually, when Mina and Jeremy were able to get back on track financially, they could spend some time finding resources for Rosie to help her cope with the trauma she experienced from being abruptly taken away from the comfort of her own home and into a new and unknown place. And while Rosie was in therapy, Jeremy and Mina worked out schedules to spend time individually with Anna and Leah. This time was rewarding because it gave them a chance to spend time with their parents one-on-one like they had never experienced before.

Furthermore, spending time with their parents meant open communication lines where they could voice their concerns. This was a space for Jeremy and Mina to patiently explain that compassion and empathy were essential traits to have, especially when someone new like Rosie enters their lives. While Anna, Leah and Rosie have grown closer and developed a sibling dynamic of their own, that isn't to say that it was an easy task by any means.

It took a collective effort from everyone's part to make the family work, which is the key takeaway from this story. A collectivized effort showed less than enthusiastic members that this was something they had to spend time working at because everyone else was doing so. Understandably, there were plenty of hiccups along the way, but as the famous African proverb goes: "It takes a village to raise a child". And the adage very much applies here to each of the children. Everyone was going through their issues that plagued the family dynamic as a whole. It took the whole family to sit down and re-evaluate their situation to make substantial changes that would benefit every family member.

For Mina, raising daughters in a family context meant identifying the most important values to the whole family. She wanted to be able to convey these values, mostly by example. It was imperative to model the values in daily life that she wanted her daughters to learn. Emulating the traits and strengths like kindness, gentleness, faithfulness, self-control, perseverance and tolerance were the qualities she wanted her daughters to develop as they grew, which is why it was so important to reflect these qualities in how she parented.

Chapter 4:
Breaking Through the Perpetual Glass Ceiling

Teen girls face countless limitations within a patriarchal society that tells them what they can or cannot do. This is the reality of what females face in the real world, and these can eventually develop into full psychological roadblocks that your children will have to face in their adulthood. As their parent, it is your responsibility to forewarn your daughters of the realities and vulnerabilities that girls have to face outside of the household. These differences between genders are further fostered when your child enters the education system, mainly seen through the many education systems that segregate boys and girls during physical education classes. While education systems differ worldwide, the school system is often where these notions of gender and the applicable stereotypes are established within your child. By the time your child has entered their teen years, ideas of "running like a girl" or "acting like a boy" have firmly wormed their way into their mindset. It is an inevitable result of the education system.

The glass ceiling is an invisible barrier that prevents women from reaching the same potential as their male counterparts. Women often feel the impact of this early on, particularly in their teen years as they are establishing their education and career.   Your daughter will immediately notice male domination the minute she enters into the real world. Rather than stifle her and scare her, be ready to fight these obstacles presented to her by being a constant support system and shoulder to cry on. Being someone, she can turn to for advice is also crucial for her when faced with difficult decisions that she has to make.

The road ahead will not be easy, especially if she enters predominantly male-dominated fields.

You may notice overlap of the following tips from the companion book entitled *Parenting Teen Boys in Today's Challenging World*. These tips are applicable regardless of your child's gender and should be seen as cardinal rules to successfully raising children. These are especially appliable in breaking the glass ceiling for girls because it establishes stability and good role models for them to model after.

Here are some ways to set your daughter up to break her way through the glass ceiling. This will prepare her to face the challenges she will encounter head-on.

1. Build self-confidence from an early age

Develop a strong sense of self from an early age within the household. With the teen years being so divisive and stress filled, being sure of oneself can significantly reduce the impact these problems can bring. Rather than raising your child as a people pleaser, teach her to stand up for what she believes in and encourage her to use her voice. The realities of society will soon shut her down and often speak over her, so relying on her self-esteem and confidence will take her far as it will require her to use her voice unabashedly. Developing this early on can make this an inherent part of who she is once she enters teenagerhood.

2. Direct your praise to her achievements, rather than appearance

Females tend to have an obsession with their view because we are always surrounded by it in society. Rather than focusing on how she looks, focus on her achievements and how she is doing academically, morally and character-wise. This does not mean that you should never compliment your daughter on her appearance, but it does mean to be conscious of the unintentional focus people tend to have on women. Establish early on that your daughter is so much more than how she looks, and her self-worth is not tied to her appearance or how conventionally beautiful she is. Establish that beauty comes in many forms. Inner beauty is most crucial as it is gold. You should clothe yourselves instead with the beauty that comes from within, the unfading beauty of a gentle and quiet spirit, which is so precious to God (1 Peter 3:4)

3. Be affectionate

Demonstrating warmth and affection to all your children equally, regardless of gender, this allows them to feel a sense of security and comfort whenever they are in your presence. This ties in with giving them the courage to share what they may be going through as affection tells them that their parents will still love them regardless of their mistakes.

4. Avoid the "boys will be boys" mentality

This dangerous mentality is often used as an excuse to brush off certain behaviours or attitudes seen in boys. Teaching your daughters that men have to be held equally accountable for their actions allows them to see consequences for inappropriate behaviours. This also ties in with a girl's self-worth, as valuing yourself means protecting yourself from people who might want to take advantage of you. In this regard, teaching girls that there is never an excuse for inappropriate behaviour encourages them to speak out and put an end to people getting away with unacceptable behaviours.

5. Be present

While parents are expected to loosen the reins, it by no means entails completely abandoning parenting altogether. You represent a guide for your child to follow and model after, even into their adult lives. Being present in their lives means continuing the relationship and bond you share, even if you may feel like they simply do not need you anymore. Particularly when your daughter is attempting to break through the glass ceiling, having the unconditional and constant support of their parents reiterates that they are doing the right thing and will always have some form of stability even if their attempts at equality fail.

6. Be a guide

Your children look to you as their role model from the minute they are brought into this world. Especially for mothers, daughters look to you to see how you fight the everyday biases imposed onto you. Model for them how you would want them to act when faced in the same situation, regardless of how young they may be. Children are inclined to mimic their parents and recreate their behaviours because it is the best reference point. This way, you provide her with solutions to everyday problems that she will inevitably face as a teen daughter. Always be extremely conscious that your children are always watching you and by the time they are teens, they will use your behaviour as an argument should you stray away from the action or attitude you are trying to impart on them.

7. Claiming worth

Form an early age, teach your daughters to evaluate their beauty and competence by their maker's terms. Your daughters will try to avoid tying their self-worth to frivolous things and terms set by other people by encouraging this. Instead, they follow the laid down standard from their maker's perspective and create their standards to live by and determine what they deserve, despite the noise that will continuously bring them down and tell them they are lesser than.

8. Embrace a growth mindset

Because teens are so susceptible to mistakes, encouraging a "growth mindset" rather than a "fixed" one teaches your kids to learn from their mistakes and treat them as a learning lesson to develop themselves. This way, rather than focusing on the fact that they were wrong, focus on what exactly they did. Should they be faced with the same situation, they will better understand how to respond appropriately. Ultimately, we are all human and while finding our purpose in life is complicated but can be made easier by studying, reading and rereading scriptures spending 1-2 minutes allows the idea of God's presence settle around one, praying back God's truths, personalizing known truth, practising God's presence by recognizing that He is with you, meditating and obeying scriptures. We are creatures that learn and can expand, diversify and grow; mentally spiritually and socially.

9. Make room for failure

Failure can be extremely disappointing at this young age because teens tend to fixate on being an outlier as they want to fit in and be part of a group. Rather than glossing over the fact that they have failed something or avoiding a discussion about it, teach them to approach it head-on to face their fears and frights and get used to confronting these uncomfortable and less than ideal aspects of life. Getting used to failing sets them up for a life of unexpected failures, and having a healthy way of coping with them from an early age will help them much in the long run.

10. Focus on extending compassion

Encourage your children to treat themselves with kindness and acceptance. Self-loathing and hatred can manifest during these early ages of teenagerhood because your kids simply don't know how to cope with everyday life pressures, their academic performance and their changing bodies. These are huge stressors that weigh your teens down heavily. Rather than focusing on what they may be achieving all the time, focus on the language they use on themselves. Teach your teens to focus on their well-being by extending the kindness they would treat others with upon themselves. Understanding that every person is flawed and that we will never please every person we meet is something that we have to grapple with and get used to from a young age.

11. Avoid comparisons

Parents sometimes feel inclined to compare our kids to how our neighbour's kids might be doing. Everyone is at different aspects of their journeys, and we have to respect that our children will go through their unique journey. Rather than comparing them to others, compare your kids with where they were last year. Encourage them by pointing out how much they have developed in character and matured. Focus on spiritual, educational and self-development in a healthy and sustainable way.

12. Social media

Platforms like Instagram can have a negative impact on the way your teen views herself and her self-worth. It also places a significant emphasis on appearance. Social media and the concept of "likes" can seriously affect your child's development and foster jealousy and envy, leading to depression and anxiety. Encourage them to take breaks away from social media by nurturing their hobbies and interests.

13. Problem-solving

Encourage your daughters to solve her issues on her own rather than fixing things for her. Parents tend to take over because of their years of experience and knowledge, but girls don't develop the coping skills they need to handle situations independently. This is the time to ask your daughter to come up with her strategies or deal with a problem, and then let her decide what she wants to do. Even if you disagree with her choice and know its incorrect, give your daughter a sense of control over her own life and show her that she is responsible for her decisions.

14. Encourage her to take physical risks.

Girls are not dainty and should be allowed to get hurt and play in the mud as boys do. By letting girls take physical risks, she will develop stronger self-esteem because she can face challenges with confidence. Encourage your daughter to go beyond her comfort zone. This can look like putting her in a new sport or encouraging her to take small risks when riding her bicycle. Give her small challenges to conquer first so that she can grow more accustomed to pushing herself. Even non-athletic girls should develop some experience when it comes to physical activity while they are young. Forming a physical relationship with their body allows them to build confidence and get to know their limits even better.

15. Avoid drama

Catty behaviour or girl fighting has been long associated with girls and high school. If you have spotted it as a parent, it's a good idea to address it immediately to nip it in the bud. Catty behaviour is immature and childish. Gossip, rumour-spreading, exclusion and physical violence like hitting are behaviours that are not tolerated and should be stopped if it ever occurs. This does not mean that all girls have a mean streak in them and automatically want to gossip pull other girls' hair. However, this is a typical behaviour found in high school that should not be encouraged by any means. Suppose you find that your daughter is engaging in this mean-spirited behaviour. In that case, it's time to have a serious sit-down about bullying and practice more positive ways to change their relationships.

Adolescence is a time filled with self-doubt, and for many teen girls, this may be a time of struggle as they view themselves with a new light of insecurities. Early on, establishing with your kids that their self-worth is not directly tied with their outward appearance is an important lesson that needs to be learnt. For your daughters to feel confident in their convictions, employ these strategies that encourage self-growth and improvement and focus on efforts rather than immediate outcomes. Teaching your daughters to be assertive and having the ability to speak up for themselves in an appropriate way that will help re-establish a sense of confidence within themselves. A teen who can speak up for themselves is also less likely to be bullied or bullied for very long because their self-worth is perceived in a different and positive light. As it has been reiterated, the best way for your kids to understand and grasp this behaviour and attitude quickly is if parents themselves model this behaviour to have a first-hand view of how confidence and self-assuredness can significantly benefit them. Facing situations with courage helps your teen in the long run.

The most challenging aspect of encouraging positive thinking is to instil in your teens to think positively about themselves. A person's inner monologue plays a critical role in how they perceive themselves, and sometimes it seems easier to criticize and pick apart every little flaw that you may see in the mirror. Rather than doing this, encourage your teens to be kind to themselves and avoid being overly harsh on themselves. Try telling them, "You would never say these cruel and unkind words to anyone else, so why is it okay to say them to yourself?" developing a healthy and positive inner monologue can be difficult because our minds automatically want to gravitate towards the negative as we notice the flaws first. But with the support of parents and open discussion about what teens may think of themselves, this is a great way to teach your children to put a positive spin on things and be more optimistic about how they perceive themselves in their environment. For example, reframe thoughts like, "I'm not capable of doing this," into something more positive like, "I'm going to try my best and learn from my mistakes."

People often underestimate how much our thoughts can affect our ability, but by simply changing the way we think, we can have a more profound and positive impact on how we end up performing. Most of the time, a positive spin is met with reluctance. But try it for yourself and see how changing your mentality can have a direct correlation to how you end up performing.

Ultimately, it lies within the parent to teach their child to love themselves for who they are and not tie their worth to the number of followers they may have on Instagram or fit into that smaller jeans size. Building self-worth on a healthy foundation is the key to its sustainability. Emphasize the essential values like kindness, compassion, empathy and respect for others as the primary benchmarks for a person's self-worth.

Chapter 5:
Breaking Stereotypes

Just like how there are many hobbies or interests that have been deemed "too girly" for men, the same can be said for women where their abilities are severely underestimated for specific activities and thus deemed unable to perform at the same standard of males. Not only is this false and an incredibly problematic generalization, but it also severely limits the capabilities of both males and females. These are great hobbies to encourage your teen girls to pursue that might seem "unconventional" but have significant mental and physical health benefits. Helping your teens build new skills redirects their focus from daily stressors like social media in a healthy and productive way.

1. Martial arts

Being able to verbally assert themselves or de-escalate a situation is a good starting point, but sometimes your teen may be in a vulnerable spot where they will have to use physical force. Learning self-defence as a young teen is particularly helpful and can potentially save your daughter's life. Aside from this, being successful in martial arts requires a high level of discipline and focus. It encourages individuals to use their physicality and improve them to grow stronger and keep your kids moving and active.

2. Fishing

Fishing is an excellent way to explore the outdoors and experience nature in an all-encompassing way. Many people choose to hike to their fishing spot, which can significantly help destress and relax them. Being out in the open of nature can be an incredible distraction from the stressors of daily life. This hobby is certainly not encouraged enough in young teens, especially girls. Fishing encourages individuals to familiarize themselves with local flora and fauna and get used to being out in the wilderness for fresh air, rather than being cooped up indoors.

3. Poker

Poker is a great way to boost your teen's concentration and observation skills. It encourages self-control as you ensure you are focused on your hand and has several cognitive benefits. It boosts mathematical skills and further develops logical thinking skills. It is an inclusive game yet is often treated as a game solely for males.

4. Woodworking

This is another hobby that encourages perseverance and focuses on creating a final product. It helps teens develop their fine motor skills and tactile side to create a project that they are proud of. If your child finds that they do not enjoy painting or pottery, consider enrolling them in woodworking activities to experience another activity that encourages creative thinking. It can be incredibly validating for your teen to say that they have made something by themselves.

5. Golf

Golf is often regarded as a male sport because it can be entirely male-dominated. But for a teen girl, this is a great sport that is challenging to master as it encourages bettering your own game. It relies on the individual developing their skill set to do better than they last did and can be a calming and relaxing activity.

6. Chess

Chess is a game that challenges a person's ability to think logically and plan. It teaches teens the basics of strategy by employing their observational and planning skills to make their move. These skills are also transferrable as they can be applied to life situations and social encounters.

7. Survival camp

These are a great summer experience for your teens to experience. Learning survival skills out in nature will teach teens lifelong skills that they otherwise will never be exposed to and in a controlled environment with instructors and peers. This is an excellent way to push the limits and test your teens' abilities against extreme adversity, alongside teamwork.

8. Music production

Get your teens to tap into their musical side and tie it in with their technical knowledge to express themselves by creating music. Music has many benefits to destress and help improve memory and mood.

9. Coding

For a long time, coding was a male-dominated field and continues to be in many ways. The gender gap does exist when it comes to coding. However, for teen girls, fostering this interest in technology and computer science can open up several career-wise pathways. Computer science is an important field that is rapidly expanding yet not enough girls are encouraged to pursue it as a career. Foster this interest from a young age.

10. Fencing

This sport teaches teens the dynamics of offence and defence while increasing coordination and agility. Another excellent way to promote cardiovascular health as fencing, while it may seem deceivingly simply, is a full-body workout that requires endurance and flexibility.

Ultimately, your teens' possibilities to pursue are endless, regardless of whether they are male or female. As a parent, it is crucial to rid ourselves of these notions that certain hobbies are "too manly" or "too feminine" for boys and girls. Rather than placing these limitations on teens, encourage them to pursue their interests wholeheartedly and dedicatedly. By doing so, you open them up to a world of endless possibilities that teaches them that there are no limits to what they can achieve.

Chapter 6:
A Personal Story

Parents worldwide have faced rough patches at some point or another with their children, no matter what gender they are. The teenage years are notorious for being particularly difficult for parents and children alike to manoeuvre. For Daniel and Lisa, parents of twins named Jessica and Jenny, parenting was seemingly a breeze until their daughters entered high school. They beat terrible twos and threes and got past kindergarten and elementary school without a hitch, much to the chagrin of their friends who were also parents but going through the opposite with their children. While they were struggling to get their children to focus on school and get over the separation anxiety of going to kindergarten, Jessica and Jenny seemed to be independent and confident and ready to tackle anything. Some might say it was because they were twins, and because of the constant companionship they had with each other allowed them to feel comfortable. Still, Daniel and Lisa chose to separate the twins in their classes very early to develop independently.

All of this went smoothly and just as expected. Feeling confident, when their daughters entered high school and began puberty, Daniel and Lisa were not expecting the problems that arose. They were undoubtedly unprepared to face everything that happened. This is often the first mistake that parents make when their children age. Being unprepared for the fact that your children are evolving and the transition from childhood to teenagerhood can happen in a blink of an eye that one day you'll find yourself faced with a teenager who talks back, pushes the boundaries more than before and knows how to get under your skin truly.

For the twins, this was a time of personal discovery and the beginnings of exploring their identity. High school meant newfound freedoms and pushing the boundary with their parents. But for Daniel and Lisa, they found themselves extremely uncomfortable and unable to handle the changes they were faced with. Jessica and Jenny began experimenting with their looks, trying out extreme hairstyles and outfits. They were hanging out with a new cohort of friends as well. But perhaps the most worrying thing for Daniel and Lisa was the fact that Jessica and Jenny began arguing and quarrelling even more than usual. Their relationship seemed to diverge the longer they spent in high school, where the fights were intense and sometimes got physical. For the parents who had never seen anything like it, they were at a loss as to what to do and how to discipline their daughters.

Every day seemed more problematic than the last as it brought more challenges and issues that either parent, who were both working full-time, were unable to cope with. Everything seemed to come to an end one day, after a long day of work and school, when an argument erupted between Jessica and Jenny.

For the two of them, sharing a bedroom had recently become a point of contention that neither Daniel nor Lisa knew how to fix. The two of them had always shared a bedroom, and there was simply no option to separate them and give them their bedrooms. The argument became too heated such that Daniel and Lisa found themselves having to separate the twins when they began to get physical.

Having children who fight is a regular thing. All siblings bicker, fight, and argue, and parents generally tend to stay out of it because usually, it can be resolved between your children. After all, the issue may not be as severe. Daniel and Lisa's case was definitely on the more extreme side of things, but not an uncommon occurrence either. That is to say, having a hands-off approach is not by any means a bad thing when it comes to letting your kids solve their little arguments. Still, sometimes you might have to be a little bit more careful and stay on top of things and what exactly your kids are arguing about because the issue might be much more severe than you may have anticipated.

The good news is that there was a happy ending for the family, as they eventually figured out the twins' problems. Unfortunately, there was no simple cure that would automatically fix everything overnight. It took weeks and weeks of therapy and very serious and long conversations with all of the parties involved to get to the problem's root. For Jessica, Daniel and Lisa found that she struggled to find her high school identity and wanted to find her independence from being a twin sister, as she was always being compared to Jenny. And for Jenny, she struggled with the anxiety and hostility from her sister and didn't know how to cope with this, aside from continually antagonizing Jessica. The problems were complex and deeply rooted in both of them, and Daniel and Lisa finally understood that they had to approach them individually. There was simply no other option but to separate them and try to solve the problem by sitting each twin down and having a long and difficult conversation with them.

This is something that parents struggle with, and Daniel and Lisa were no exception. Understanding that your child is a person and having very mature and intense emotions is one of the first things to grapple with as you watch your child grow before your eyes. While not all parents will have a set of twins and the same circumstances, Jessica and Jenny's problems are by no means unique to them. Teens worldwide struggle with their mental health every day, and parents must stay proactive and involved in their children's' lives.

Perhaps the most helpful tip that Daniel and Lisa would want to impart onto other parents struggling to strike a balance in their parenting is to build a solid foundation early on in their kids' lives. The values that you instil in your children cannot be built overnight. This is something that has to be practised and preached from day one. You may ask how this helps with parenting teenagers? The fact is that this has everything to do with parenting your teen because this period in their lives is full of uncertainties that most teens resort to hiding from their parents. They lie and omit details for fear of punishment. Yet the crucial part from Daniel and Lisa's story is that even though it took a while, their daughters eventually came around and felt confident in their ability to share the details of their troubles with their parents so that they could seek help from them. From childhood, you should be implementing most of these tips to set you up for a solid foundation by the time they reach teenagerhood.

- Open communication lines: They say "honesty is the best policy". be open and honest with your children. This rule should be held to a high regard because lying to your kids will only backfire at some point. Not only that, but you are teaching them that deception and deceit are allowed. It's always important to differentiate between what you say out of necessity (for example, for safety) and lying with ill intent. This is crucial when it comes time for your child to open up to you. You will want your child to understand that being honest is a good and virtuous thing.

- Listen: While talking to your daughter is so important, knowing when to listen is equally just as crucial. As much as you will want to lecture your daughter while she expresses all of the mistakes she's made, carefully assess the situation to see if she has learned her lesson and go from there. If you recognize that she has internalized her mistakes and grown from it, take the time to listen carefully to what she is saying, rather than preparing your next lecture.

- Talk about *neutral* topics: As much as you want your child to be able to open up to you with their deepest, darkest secrets, remember that it's also important to talk about other aspects of life too, like what might be going on in their lives, how the school is, their passions and maybe even your desires also. Neither of you are robots, so it's important not to approach building a relationship robotically. Instead of being hyper-focused on the fact that you *want* to build a relationship, focus on what you and your child are talking about.

- Create new memories: As much as having a daily routine with kids is very crucial, and sometimes you may not have the luxury to travel and do extravagant things, getting away and trying something new with your kids is so important. Making new memories does not have to be an exceptionally elaborate and expensive thing. It can be as simple as a ritual like Sunday brunches or going to the museum or even a movie night. These little things help build a strong foundation because it shows your child that you are first and foremost, interested in their lives, and you want to spend time with them.

- Encourage participation: Everyone in the family must practice these habits. By doing so with parents and all of your kids, this develops it into something automatic and done without prompting, which is precisely where these roots of trust begin. Your child opening up to you should never feel like a chore for them or you, so when it becomes an automatic thing that does not fill them with dread and is simply a part of the day, you know you are doing something correctly.

- Share the load: Remember that it takes a village to raise children, so ensure that the whole family is involved in building that solid foundation. You might find that your attempts are not as successful as you like, but perhaps another parent, a grandparent or even an aunt might be having more luck with talking to your child. That is not to say that this is your chance to give up. Instead, this is your chance to try harder to understand what your child is going through and empathize with them even more.

- Make the most out of opportunities that present themselves: The car ride home is an excellent place to have a conversation with your child in a calm and non-threatening environment. Discuss topics that are easy and natural to both of you. Take these small windows of private time to get to know your teen.

- Take advantage of the environment: This tip goes hand in hand with the previous advice but a good time to have a conversation with your child is at nighttime. Bedtime should be a calm and chilled out environment, thus making your child feel at ease and away from the stress of everyday life, which you might probably reflect as well. Building a calm environment can be difficult, so take note of times where you can simply just sit and relax and have a conversation with your child.

- Be brave: A surprising thing that many parents face is fear and indecisiveness in talking to their children. For many, it can seem like a daunting task. But the first step to overcoming this is not to see this as a task, but one of the joys that is part of parenting. Understanding that your child is also human and has their independent thoughts can lead to some very enlightening and exciting conversations if you let it happen.

- Stay committed: It can be an easy thing to do once and then forget all of these habits soon after. The truth is that you must implement these practices in your daily life and keep at it for the long run. This is how these values develop at a young age and stick around at crucial years like teenagerhood and when your kids reach the young adult age.

As much as parents might think that building a solid foundation is an easy thing to do, sometimes it can be far more challenging than you may have expected because life is incredibly unpredictable. You can never know what unexpected circumstances might keep you away from your child, and you never know what life may throw at you. As your children age, they get increasingly busy. Many parents end up struggling to find any time at all in their schedules or in their children's programs to sit down and talk to get to know each other, which can be so tricky when you want to understand your child as a human being truly. Bearing this in mind, it's crucial to find every opportunity you can to show your child that you love them and want to spend time with them. Your interest and enthusiasm itself can genuinely show your kids that it's not always about gifts or expensive vacations. For them, seeing your small efforts prove to be far more effective than anything else.

Chapter 7:
Teens in the World

The scariest part for parents to come to terms with when their kids are teenagers is the fact that they are not around them 24/7, meaning their kids are spending increasing amounts outside of the house and more importantly, outside of parents' radar. This is the scariest part about your child growing and maturing into teenagerhood because for them. It means increased time outside of the home with a later curfew. For parents, this means more opportunities to get into trouble, to be in danger and be faced with temptations and the harsh realities of the world that you have fought so hard to shield and protect them from.

The first thing to understand is that your children are no longer blank slates. At some point, they have to experience the real world and all of the difficult things that come with it. Protecting your children from these things is essential, but completely neglecting to inform your kids about ugly things in life like abuse, terrorism, genocide, and some other scary but very real topics are merely setting your children up for a very rude awakening.

The fact is, as much as you want to protect them from all of the harsh realities of the world, doing so is just impossible because eventually, your child will have to face it all. Ultimately, you would much rather your children be able to handle all of these negative and scary things that the world presents.

However, what happens when your teen is just beginning to navigate through the world and is faced with alcohol and drugs? How does a parent prepare their children about the dangers that can potentially lead to even worse and harmful circumstances that might even affect the rest of their lives? This is a giant pill for parents to swallow, and a topic that many parents neglect entirely to breach because it can be incredibly intimidating for both parents and children. But it is essential. Not only for your children but perhaps their peers and friends as well, should your child have the courage to speak up when faced with a difficult decision like this.

The last chapter focused on building trust with your kids. This is the foundational basis for all of the parenting. No matter what, you must trust your children, and they must trust you. This is the only way to truly get your message across and for them to have the respect and thoughtfulness to listen to what you are saying and truly absorb the information. For many teens, things go in one ear and out the other, especially where their parents are concerned. But if you approach the subject as something incredibly serious, which it is, and convey that this needs their undivided attention, you are at a good starting point to have a serious sit-down about what your kids get up to when you are not around.

Ultimately, this is not an interrogation, so be sure not to treat it as such. Treat your child as the adult that they are about to be. Teenagerhood is all about recognizing and validating that your child is growing into their independence and finding their own in the world, so be sure to treat them as such. Once you have them in the right place to broach the subject, it can be as simple as asking them what they know about drugs and alcohol. Provided that you have the trust built between the two of you and you've followed some of the tips from Chapter 6, hopefully, your child will open up about the topic. Many teens will tread extra carefully for fear of punishment or discipline, even if they haven't dabbled in any of the substances.

Remember, this is not an interrogation. Be watchful of their mood changing or any guards going up. Perhaps your teen gets defensive. Remember that you are here to give them the advice and education they need, not dole out more punishments. This is where you acknowledge that they may have come in contact with substances and calmly educate them about why underage drinking and smoking are extremely dangerous and can seriously affect their health and their future should they get caught and even if they are not caught the bigger eye is watching.

For teens, drugs and alcohol are an exciting thing, mostly because it is so heavily frowned upon and beyond that, completely illegal. For many, the adrenaline rush of doing something wrong can get them going and making stupid decisions that will negatively impact their lives, should it go on a criminal record of some kind. This is why parents need to take an active role in educating their children and providing them with an out should they ever be caught in a position where they are too afraid to resist or say no.

Giving your teens a rundown of what they might encounter while they are not under adult supervision is a good idea. Teaching them how to spot drugs or alcohol is an excellent step to get them to steer clear of it and perhaps get out of the situation just in time.

There are multiple ways to approach this. You can tell your teen to call or text you, or perhaps a trusted older sibling/cousin/whatever the case is. As much as you want to give your teen the freedom to go out to that get-together, you also want to provide them with a way out that won't get them in trouble. It is crucial to tell your kids that they will not get in trouble for seeking help. Punishing your kids when they have found themselves in a sticky situation and have sought help is a sure way to make sure they will never make use of this exit ever again.

Practice lines with your teens to get them out of these situations, like coming up with excuses. These can be as simple as, "I have health issues" or "I can't come home under the influence, my parents will notice". It may take some practice but coming up with a realistic way can protect your teens from potential harm. And ultimately, for parents, the most important thing is that their children are safe and away from danger.

Trusting your teens to be on their own is a natural part of them growing up. The most important thing that you can do to make sure that they do not get into trouble is to educate them on how and why certain things are wrong and lead to severe consequences that even you, the parent, cannot protect them from. While you do not want to scare your teens and traumatize them from ever going out again, it is essential to teach them about finding the right friends who positively influence them and want the best for them, rather than being focused on ruining their futures. By instilling this early on, your child will be able to spot out manipulators and cheaters from their young age and will carry the lesson with them for the rest of their lives.

Focus on the fact that what they do when Mum and Dad are away are solely their responsibility. Instilling in your teens that actions can have incredibly grave consequences can be scary for them, but it is a reality that they have to face to grow and mature. This is merely another natural part of growing up and becoming a full-grown teenager, where you are faced with the not-so-nice realities of the world. Your teenagers are no longer children, and now, another set of rules, responsibilities and expectations are placed on them because growing older is not always fun and games.

Girls are more prone to be affected later in life by a past hurting memory. Whether it is effects of bullying, low self-esteem, mental health struggles or a combination of all of them, these issues will always return to haunt your daughter if left undealt with and untreated. It can create an incredibly dangerous circumstance for your daughter. Issues can leave a deep and permanent fissure on your daughter's personality. Mothers usually come in here to help their teen daughters face these issues by encouraging them to lean on their shoulder and share these burdens that are weighing heavily on their minds.

For Luna, her mother Diana was extremely perceptive over her child's switch in moods. She noticed almost immediately that her daughter was coming home from school subdued. Luna was not eating as much as she used to and was more recluse, spending increasing amounts of time alone and away from her friends. This was shocking for Diana, who was incredibly used to seeing her daughter surrounded by friends, and family. This was a clear indicator that her daughter was experiencing some difficult times.

In high school, girls tend to move in cliques and close-up units that keep secrets, which can be dangerous for innocent young girls. Diana felt like her role here was to discern what was bothering her daughter. Diana had to do some sleuthing that went behind Luna's back as she tried to figure out what was going on with her daughter through her friends. Word got back around to Luna, who was furious.

After a blowout argument that resulted in tears, Diana had the chance to calmly explain her side and show her daughter that she did what she had to do to figure out how to help her because she was so closed-off from her. Diana could express her most vulnerable feelings to her daughter, who finally saw that her mother truly just wanted to help her. Unlike the clique of girls at school who was only pretending to be her friend so that they could cheat off of her during tests, Diana was someone who would not merely get rid of her because she was bored or no longer useful to Luna. The blow on Luna's self-esteem was immense. But together with Diana, they were able to work through the bullies' negative comments to begin to mend and heal from the trauma slowly.

Years later, Luna would still have social anxieties that were rooted in her experiences from high school. It would scar her permanently, and social situations with groups of people became a new challenge she would have to tackle when entering the workforce. And Luna is by no means an exception to this. Plenty of people have experienced some trauma that was left unresolved from their childhood or teenage years. The difference here is that Luna was able to admit that she was struggling with her mother from a young age and work at it until she could cope healthily by the time she was an adult.

In some cases, girls may instead prefer to talk to their fathers than their mothers when facing difficulties. Regardless of who they choose, it is essential to develop trust between everyone involved.

Some tips for fathers raising daughters:

1. How you talk to and treat women will have a lasting impact on how your daughter perceives herself. Your daughter will be wise to the stereotypes and negative view you may have on other women. Her identity is shaped by what it is to be a woman and growing up with a father who respects women shows her how to expect to be treated. Be positive and respectful. Avoid using foul language that puts down females.

2. Honesty and integrity in relationships are vital factors for a healthy and happy future. Demonstrate this to her to have a healthy relationship model to look to when examining her future relationships. Show her that just because her mum is not with you due to various reasons does not mean you will compromise the essential values. It also shows that you should be consistent with the qualities and values that are most important in your own life.

3. Include her. Fathers often feel like their daughters are not capable or too fragile to do "manly" things like play football. But the fact is that hobbies are not assigned by gender. Interests are simply that, just interests. So, involve your daughter in your favourite hobbies because she's only as capable as the next person. And before you know it, she might even have a knack for it and do better than you.

4. Similarly, if your daughter wants to be girly, allow her to do so. You don't have to force her into dresses she does not like if she does not want to wear them, just because she is a girl. Allow her to express herself as freely as she wants without fear of being reprimanded. (This helps to know her way of thinking)

5. Don't avoid uncomfortable talks just because you are different genders. Ultimately, if the conversation is about biology, you just have to get it over with. It should never be a taboo subject or treated as such. Try your best to accept that this is reality and have an adult conversation with your daughter.

When it comes to helping your daughters develop and grow as individuals, mothers tend to relate as they may have undergone the same experiences growing up themselves. That is not to say, however, that mothers can be the only guide for daughters. This can vary depending on the individual. Perhaps an older sibling, an aunt or even a cousin might provide some guidance to someone who is lost or experiencing hardship. While Luna was lucky and had her mother to turn to, many people do not have that privilege and instead have to turn to other figures in their lives.

- Regardless of your relationship, here are some helpful tips for nurturing in teen girls.

Like the saying goes: "Like mother, like daughter". This tends to happen because mothers can only give what they are made of. Mothers can only share their own experiences to relate to their daughters, which usually ends up in many similarities shared between both mother and daughter.

- Love her and show her affirmations as a person.

Too often are girls' self-worth tied to things like beauty or grades. Instead of doing so, value the person she is on the inside and the good qualities that make her important, what she loves, and values. Rather than see her as lesser than because she is not a certain weight or wears a specific style of clothes, place higher importance on her mind, passions, and the type of person she emulates.

- Do not accuse or condemn her for her own decisions. Never judge her for the choices she makes, even if they end up being mistakes. These serve as huge learning lessons for her that she will take with her for the rest of her life. These are also lessons that you might not be able to give her, and the only way for her to truly learn is by doing so on her own. Instead of being a voice of constant critique and criticism, empathize and be compassionate towards her plights and try to offer as much comfort as you possibly can.

- Be courteous and interested in her person and what concerns her.

Your daughter has her passions and interests that have shaped her into who she is. Her interests could be "manly" things like sports or video games, but that does not mean she should be limited from them just because of a societal perception. Respect her interests and take them as seriously as she would take them. Parents often make remarks that can cut deeper than they realize. Instead of doing this, remember to be respectful and treat your daughter as you would want others to treat her.

- Be considerate with her and discipline in love, rather than in anger.

Providing a clear explanation of what she has done wrong and how it could have negatively impacted her life is a point that is crucial to get across when dealing with a wayward teenager who is rebelling and continuously breaking the rules. Be firm and consistent with punishments and be sure to explain *why* she is facing the penalties. Fairness is fundamental to teens, and unfair punishment can lead to festering resentment towards authority. Your teen might be more tempted to rebel and evade any forms of control because no one treats them like an adult.

Chapter 8:
"Decoding" Your Teens and Helping Them Thrive

Thriving teens can be a more daunting task than a parent may have expected. As your teen is trying to find their way through the hustle and bustle of school, extracurriculars and friends, it can certainly be challenging to feel like they are growing and thriving as a person. For parents, here are some tips to help your teen ease into this new stage in life.

-   Schooling: Stay on top of your teen's education. This can be an extremely volatile time that sees a lot of grades slipping. While marks aren't everything in life, they can undoubtedly indicate how your teen handles all of their responsibilities and newfound pressures that they suddenly have to deal with. If you have determined that your child is struggling with school, this may be the right time to find a tutor or take extra time with your teens if you help them with homework. The key is to show them that there is always room for improvement and how to work at something with discipline and patience to grasp a concept and excel at it genuinely.

- Talents: Your child is unique in every way and may have an exceptional mastery of their own. Whether its music or math, finding ways to truly nurture these talents and encourage your teen to find a passion or a hobby that they excel in is a great way to not only teach them how to spend their time productively, but it also shows them that investing in yourself is so vital to improving yourself. Here, show them that nurturing their talents is a worthwhile cause because it brings joy and educates them on new and unique things that exist in the world that they may not have been exposed to before.

- Sleep: Humans needs sleep to thrive as human beings. For teens, the temptation is to stay awake up until the wee hours of the morning on their phone or computer. This can have long-lasting effects later on in life, not to mention severely affecting cognition and alertness during the daytime. Be sure to encourage your children to take advantage of sleep and perhaps even impose discipline over phone use if the addiction gets too overwhelming for both parents and teens alike. Furthermore, this is also an excellent chance to have a conversation about how texting and the lack of face-to-face contact might be severely hindering your child's interactions and socializing.

- Reading: Reading is one of the best hobbies because it continues to educate and entertain people worldwide. It is a great activity that gets your teens away from their phones and more importantly, can really exercise imagination, thinking, and even help with their mental health. There are plenty of great benefits to reading. The best part is that with a library card (which is usually free or priced at a low cost), your teen will have access to thousands of books and resources to expand their horizons. Giving your teens books to read will change their perspectives and engage their brain into thinking in a more dynamic way.

- Enriching events: Throwing an event for your teen does not always have to be exorbitantly expensive, nor does it have to be incredibly complex and challenging to do. The important thing here to remember is that these events can significantly contribute to your teen's happiness. Making a day like a birthday or graduation into a simple event can motivate your teens and get them to approach ageing and to mature a little bit differently than simply just dreading it, as many do. Truly making someone happy on a day like this requires thoughtfulness, rather than an infinite amount of money and resources. Knowing your child and what they love is the key to making an event special for them.

- "Decoding" girls: The general approach for girls has been to decode them when this in and of itself is an inaccurate assessment for understanding girls. Girls and boys are equally just as complex, and it takes a lot of effort to truly get to know a person and understand their point of view and where they are coming from. Regardless of their gender, every person is different and has gone through their own set of experiences. To truly get to know your child and help them thrive in this world, understand them as the individual that they are, rather than gender stereotypes.

- Empowerment: Parents struggle with empowering their kids and finding the right things to say. But when it comes to genuinely empowering your kids and teaching them how to see their full worth to reach their full potential, it lies in parents to be a coach and cheer them on. Once kids see their value through their parents' eyes and witness the fact that their parents will always have faith and believe in them, they will be able to feel empowered in their skin truly.

- Motivation: As much as you might believe in your kids' abilities, progress lies in their hands where they need to feel the pull of motivation and discipline to complete their tasks and put in the work and energy they need to give whatever it is they seek to excel at. For parents, while you are your child's biggest cheerleader, a lot of motivation lies in an individual's ability to come up with it themselves. Sometimes you might need to take a step back and give your teen some space to figure out what they are working towards and then guide them and provide the support they need. It takes a lot of balancing and trial and error to truly reach a point where you meet your child's needs and don't push the boundaries with overenthusiasm.

- Bonding: Developing a special bond with your child can help push them up and reach their fullest potential. While every case is different, daughters tend to gravitate towards their mothers, while sons tend to gravitate towards their fathers. Again, this is a vast generalization, and every family's specificities can completely differ from this. Regardless of your family's circumstances, having a close bond between a parent and a teen can genuinely make all the difference in motivating and empowering them. For girls, this tends to be an excellent opportunity to talk to Mom about body image and sexuality. The same goes for boys and their fathers. This can serve as an ideal outlet for your kids to vent and rant and come to you with any questions and concerns. Ultimately, it is genuinely based on you and your own family and the configuration of parents and children.

- Discipline: While your teens are starting to look like adults and might be coming into their own, they certainly may not act like it. This is where parents and discipline come in. Regardless of how you choose to discipline your teens, they will not be happy about it. When you encounter this case, it is essential to explain to your teens why they are faced with consequences. The appropriate disciplinary tactics for a teen usually revolve around taking away privileges like cellphone use or a shortened curfew.

- Focus: Focus goes hand in hand with motivation and empowerment, but one thing to note here is that having a compass when you are a teenager can be especially difficult because teens do not know what they want to do with their lives. Expecting teenagers to figure out a career focus and the rest of their trajectory for their education is a Herculean task. But this is where parents come in. Discussing things with your teens to help them figure out their future is one of the best things you can provide your teens with because this means honesty, endless advice, and constant reassurance that your teenager is never alone.

Lisa noticed her daughter Amy's personal life was getting increasingly attractive as she aged. By her teenage years, Lisa realized it was time to have a serious talk about relationships, and it was now or never. Lisa reminded herself that while some teens will start dating earlier than others, it's completely normal to have romantic interests during the teenage years. Amy was outspoken about her interests in dating while her friends tended to keep it to themselves. Regardless of how your teen perceives the subject, don't be afraid to begin a discussion because several vital topics need to be discussed and clear ground rules that Lisa had to set.

Lisa needed to coach her daughter on handling relationships, starting with her class friends. She provided some tips at the beginning that ended up being a gateway to open Amy up and continuously keep her Mum in the loop when there are new developments in her life. Lisa quickly explained to her daughter that relationships are a commitment and the importance of getting to know someone before committing to a relationship with them.

Lisa didn't allow her to lose sight of the important things, she was aware that relationships were not the end to life, but a lifestyle that makes her maker happy is essential. At one point, though, Amy reminded herself not to neglect other aspects of life like family and extracurriculars etc. But with Lisa checking in with her daughter regularly, Amy was able to see that other aspects of life were just as important that she had to give her energy towards. Lisa was always letting her daughter know that if she ever has any questions or concerns, she could always turn to her for support or advice.

One of the areas where Lisa saw that Amy was becoming too obsessed was with her technology usage. Once she began having more friends at school, Amy's usage increased by a ten-fold where Lisa previously thought it was not possible. Having more friends was an extremely new and exciting time for Amy, so she was enthusiastic about spending time with whoever calls her. Amy wanted to text and call almost every hour of every day. It took a serious discussion between Lisa and Amy on safe practices online and not compromising herself for others and being responsible for technology use.

One of the essential things that Lisa instilled was talk about consent, which she made a big deal because it is. Consent is so necessary at any age but especially when you are young. Lisa was able to articulate to her daughter that she did not have to do anything. She could say no. Amy understood how to set her terms in her friendships and boundaries while also acknowledging others' limitations. Lisa took the time to warn Amy of things that are simply unacceptable and red flags in relationships like signs of a person being manipulated, abused, or isolated from other friends and family.

Lisa was able to find opportunities to meet her daughter's friends. There is nothing wrong with wanting to know who your child is friends with, so Lisa made herself known to all her daughter's friends. If Amy was going out, Lisa was sure to ask where they would be going and curfew times. She got acquainted with all her friends, not only for her daughter's safety but also to show that she genuinely cared about the goings-on in her daughter's life.

While you want to stay on top of everything that is going on in your child's life, privacy is equally important. While Lisa was nervous about letting her daughter out with her friends, she trusted her daughter. She knew that she was responsible enough to do so because they were regularly communicating and keeping each other up to date. Despite the growing independence, Amy is still very young. However, Lisa gave her some privacy by avoiding the urge to listen in on phone calls or eavesdrop on them. You want to maintain a balance of keeping tabs on them without being too invasive.

Lastly, if your teen is going over to their friend's house, know who is at home at the other person's house. It was important for Lisa to find out who would be home, and she took it another step further by having a quick conversation with their parents about their rules and expectations for behaviour and conduct. These were all healthy measures. Lisa, as a parent took, which she felt was allowed to take to protect her daughter.

Chapter 9:
Raising Daughters

As the other chapters have mentioned, you must see your children as the individuals they are, rather than stereotypes or generalizations that you might have heard. Daniel and Lisa from Chapter 6 learned this the hard way and found themselves faced with their family almost falling apart because they could not get their daughters to come together and figure out their problems.

So, there is no one size fits all rule that will automatically instil all of the best parenting tactics for you to grow your daughters with when it comes to raising daughters. It indeed does lie within you knowing your daughter emotionally and mentally.

This is a daunting task for parents, among many others, because how does one honestly go about getting to know their daughters and helping them grasp their internal and external identities?

One of the most significant pressures that parents face is knowing that they are always under surveillance by their children. But this is one of the most effective ways for your kids to understand how to carry themselves, particularly girls who will eventually become women. Seeing how Mom, in particular, handles herself and maintains her attitude is a guide for your daughters to do the same as they age and find themselves in various social situations.

Finding identity in a world of social media is incredibly difficult, especially for a young and impressionable mind like that of a teen girl. As a parent, it is crucial that you show your children how fake and artificial the online world can be and explain to her the sheer fact that most pictures have likely been altered and edited. Identity itself is a complicated thing that most women genuinely do not begin to even understand until adulthood. But when you are a teenager, you are forced to confront your identity quickly because the people around you want to understand you and relate to you. So for a teenage girl who is faced with the pressures of the people around her and the unrealistic standards of beauty that exist online, this can be detrimental and time and time again, this has been proven to be deadly.

Body dysmorphia and eating disorders are rampant in young girls today, and parents have to do their best to attempt even to begin to understand it and explain it to their daughters (and sons). Parents must use these formative years to instil a strong sense of self by reiterating that a person's worth is never based on their looks and adhering to beauty standards that are unrealistic and always subject to change.

Raising emotionally intelligent children is the best way to get your daughter to treat her body and mind healthily. The key to an emotionally intelligent child is teaching them how to handle negative emotions healthily. Showing kids from the minute you begin disciplining them how to recognize and deal with big feelings is the key to preventing misbehaviour — and this is a skill that will serve them their entire lives, especially when they hit teenagerhood and are faced with situations that they would never have anticipated. Being unable to handle emotions leads to more misbehaviour, trouble socially or even self-esteem problems.

The steps are simple: accept your child's feelings, and from there, it becomes a matter of guiding them through emotional moments and helping them find a solution to their problem. Sounds simple enough, right? The fact is that it can get more complicated than that. Especially when your kids become teenagers, and they disagree with most things that you say. Teenagerhood sees your child wanting to be more and more like an adult, which means ignoring all of your guidance and figuring out their path.

So what is a parent supposed to do in this situation? The best thing to do at this stage is to know where their boundaries lie and respect them. This does not mean that you have no voice in the situation; ultimately, you can choose to interject wherever you like. But the fact is that your teen will want to figure things out for themselves until they can no longer do so.

When it comes to tying in this newfound independence that your child is going through coupled with severe problems like self-esteem and self-image, finding the balance of respecting your teen's boundaries while also being concerned for their wellbeing can be extremely difficult. This is your chance to employ some of the essential tactics like listening and being a source of comfort for your kids as they try to make sense of what is going on with their bodies.

When it comes to a teen's self-esteem, focus on them as a whole person, rather than being hyper-focused on their appearance, leading to even more self-consciousness and self-loathing. There are some things you can let your child know that you are proud of; like her sense of humour, grades in school, or any other particular skill that is relevant to your child. This is also where the importance of finding fulfilment in hobbies and passions come into play. Praising your daughter for her abilities in her favourite sport, for example, is a healthier way to approach motivating and empowering her, rather than being so focused on a person's looks all of the time.

As has been mentioned previously, you are your child's most immediate and most significant role model. Developing confidence for your own body and showing that you feel positive about your own body will make it far easier for your teen to be optimistic about their own body. Having a positive attitude can be challenging to take on, but this also means avoiding things like fad or crash diets, making healthy eating and physical activity part of your everyday family life, appreciating your abilities that you are capable of with your body, having pride for yourself and extending this pride to other people and how you value them based on their qualities, rather than appearance. Be careful about subtle comments that might appear harmless but can genuinely affect someone. Commenting on someone's weight is never a good idea, whether the intent was right or not. Weight is an incredibly personal thing that every person has to struggle with. Making observations out loud is disrespectful but can also be difficult for a person to hear, especially since we can never honestly know everything a person is going through.

The best course of action is to have a serious conversation with your child about the changes they are experiencing with their body. However, many teenagers feel uncomfortable with this idea, even if you have built up a solid foundation for your relationship with your child. Sometimes the best course of action is to consult a therapist and see a professional to deal with these issues.

Teens are egomaniacs during this period, which means that you will be facing a lot of attitude and them even crossing the line in terms of behaviour. During this time, teens are hyper-focused on their problems and their desires. Teens may display selfish behaviour, but the critical thing to remember here is not to take any of it personally.

But just because bad behaviour is expected, it does not mean that this should go unpunished either. Teenagers can be extremely rude, obnoxious, and can cross the line into disrespect very quickly. They know how to push your buttons and rile you up. But as mentioned in the previous chapters, instead of getting into an argument or allowing your daughter to escalate the situation, just say, "You aren't allowed to speak to me like that. We can talk when you're going to be respectful." Perhaps taking away a privilege like their cellphone will teach them that bad behaviour has consequences. But the most important thing is for you to stay calm and remember that your teen will continue to test you and push the boundaries even further. The worst thing you can do in this situation is to give them the silent treatment or hold a grudge for too long because they are also susceptible during this time. Having an adult conversation is better than scaring them or arguing.

Please Leave a Review!

I would be incredibly thankful if you could take just 60 seconds to write a brief review on the platform of purchase, even if it's just a few sentences!

Conclusion

While there are inherent biological differences between males and females, raising them lies in parents' hands to present them with all of the opportunity they can, regardless of gender. While society may insist on enforcing these strict gender norms, as the parent, you certainly do not have to and can instead choose to view your child as the unique individual they are and foster their personal preferences, hobbies and interests.

Always keep in mind to respect your children and their rights. Respecting their identity and evolution as they try to find themselves in this complex world can be a daunting thing for teens. It serves as another form of added stress, but when armed with their parents' support, the encouragement can genuinely build their self-confidence and love that they feel towards themselves.

While teen girls face a different set of challenges than teen boys, many of the techniques and methods of coping with this from a parent's point of view overlap and can be used interchangeably as there is no "one size fit all" approach raising kids. Understand that every child is unique, and it is a responsibility of the parents to recognize what makes their child different and act on it, instead of forcing them to conform to the status quo. This can be incredibly dangerous and force your children to close themselves off from parents to the point where you will have no idea about what they may be going through.

The cardinal rule that has been continuously reiterated throughout this series of books is that unconditional love should be the backbone of parenting. You should be able to strike a balance through trial and error of the different techniques offered in this book to find one that best suits your child to foster their development as an authoritative figure while also maintaining a strong foundation and bond with your kids that allows them to feel comfortable with sharing what may be going on in their lives.

Striking this balance is possibly the greatest challenge of raising kids. While teens can present a new series of challenges and frustrations, it is still important to note that raising your kids through this new stage of life can be incredibly validating and rewarding as you witness your children grow and mature into young adults who are trying to find their place in the world and make their impact. As these books consistently discuss the difficulties parents face when raising their kids, it is crucial to point out that raising children is an immense joy and a privilege that not all people get to experience, regardless of how desperately they may want to.

Other Books You'll Love!

1. Raising Boys in Today's Digital World: Proven Positive Parenting Tips for Raising Respectful, Successful and Confident Boys

2. Raising Girls in Today's Digital World: Proven Positive Parenting Tips for Raising Respectful, Successful and Confident Girls

3. Raising Kids in Today's Digital World: Proven Positive Parenting Tips for Raising Respectful, Successful and Confident Kids

4. The Child Development and Positive Parenting Master Class 2-in-1 Bundle: Proven Methods for Raising Well-Behaved and Intelligent Children, with Accelerated Learning Methods

5. Parenting Teens in Today's Challenging World 2-in-1 Bundle: Proven Methods for Improving Teenagers Behaviour with Positive Parenting and Family Communication

6. Life Strategies for Teenagers: Positive Parenting, Tips and Understanding Teens for Better Communication and a Happy Family

7. Parenting Teen Girls in Today's Challenging World: Proven Methods for Improving Teenagers Behaviour with Whole Brain Training

8. Parenting Teen Boys in Today's Challenging World: Proven Methods for Improving Teenagers Behaviour with Whole Brain Training

9. 101 Tips For Helping With Your Child's Learning: Proven Strategies for Accelerated Learning and Raising Smart Children Using Positive Parenting Skills

10. 101 Tips for Child Development: Proven Methods for Raising Children and Improving Kids Behavior with Whole Brain Training

11. Financial Tips to Help Kids: Proven Methods for Teaching Kids Money Management and Financial Responsibility

12. Healthy Habits for Kids: Positive Parenting Tips for Fun Kids Exercises, Healthy Snacks, and Improved Kids Nutrition

13. Mini Habits for Happy Kids: Proven Parenting Tips for Positive Discipline and Improving Kids' Behavior

14. Good Habits for Healthy Kids 2-in-1 Combo Pack: Proven Positive Parenting Tips for Improving Kids Fitness and Children's Behavior

Facebook Community

I will like to invite you to our Facebook community group to visit this link and join group. https://www.facebook.com/groups/397683731371863

This is a private group where parents, teachers and carers can learn, share tips, ask questions, discuss and get valuable content about raising and parent modern children. It is a very supportive and encouraging group where valuable content, free resources and exciting discussion about parenting is being shared. You can use this to benefit from social media. You will be learning a lot from school teachers, experts, counsellors, new and experienced parents, and stay updated with our latest releases.

See you there!

References

[1] https://cchp.ucsf.edu/sites/g/files/tkssra181/f/SelfEsteem_en0710.pdf

[2] https://www.theseus.fi/bitstream/handle/10024/50239/Anttila_Marianna_Saikkonen_Pinja.pdf

[3] https://ijcat.com/archives/volume5/issue2/ijcatr05021006.pdf

[4] https://www.harvey.k-state.edu/family-and-consumer-sciences/family_and_child_development/documents/CommunicatingwTeenTrust.pdf

[5] https://www.researchgate.net/publication/283721084_Early_Reading_Development

[6] https://www.understood.org/en/friends-feelings/empowering-your-child/building-on-strengths/download-hands-on-activity-to-identify-your-childs-strengths

[7]
https://www.wfm.noaa.gov/pdfs/ParentingYourTeen_Hando ut1.pdf
[8] https://www.helpguide.org/articles/depression/parents-guide-to-teen-depression.htm?pdf=13027
[9]
https://www2.ed.gov/parents/academic/help/adolescence/a dolescence.pdf
[10]
http://centerforchildwelfare.org/kb/prprouthome/Helping%2 0Your%20Children%20Navigate%20Their%20Teenage%20Ye ars.pdf
[11]
https://www.childrensmn.org/images/family_resource_pdf/0 27121.pdf
[12]
https://educationnorthwest.org/sites/default/files/developing -empathy-in-children-and-youth.pdf
[13] http://drkateaubrey.com/wp-content/uploads/2016/02/Parenting-Your-Strong-Willed-Child.pdf
[14]
https://www.researchgate.net/publication/263227023_Family _Time_Activities_and_Adolescents'_Emotional_Well-being
[15] https://parenting-ed.org/wp-content/themes/parenting-ed/files/handouts/communication-parent-to-child.pdf
[16] https://www.wikihow.mom/Trust-Your-Teenager

[17]
https://www.statmodel.com/download/Meeus,%20vd%20Sc hoot,%20Klimstra%20&.pdf

[18]
https://www.nap.edu/resource/19401/ProfKnowCompFINAL. pdf

[19]
http://www.delmarlearning.com/companions/content/141801 9224/AdditionalSupport/box11.1.pdf

[20]
http://resources.beyondblue.org.au/prism/file?token=BL/1810 _A

[21] https://exeter.anglican.org/wp-content/uploads/2014/11/Listening-to-children-leaflet_NCB.pdf

[22]
https://www.researchgate.net/publication/312600262_Creati ve_Thinking_among_Preschool_Children

[23] https://www.gutenberg.org/files/15114/15114-pdf.pdf

[24]
https://discovery.ucl.ac.uk/id/eprint/1522668/1/Thesis%20M oulton%20V%20281016.pdf

[25]
https://www.bda.uk.com/foodfacts/healthyeatingchildren.pd f

[26]

http://www.tuskmont.org/uploads/1/7/7/2/17728377/follow_the_child_trust_the_child.pdf

[27] https://www.apa.org/pi/families/resources/develop.pdf

[28]

https://extension.colostate.edu/docs/pubs/consumer/10249.pdf

[29] https://www.empoweringparents.com/article/risky-teen-behavior-can-you-trust-your-child-again/

[30]

http://www.wecf.eu/download/2018/05%20May/WSSPPublicationENPartC-MHMchapter.pdf

Milton Keynes UK
Ingram Content Group UK Ltd.
UKHW020636230124
436534UK00016B/590